Silence

*Ways to Be Silent
Before the Lord*

Come and sit a while...

Silence in His Presence:

Ways to Be Silent Before the Lord

Come sit a while . . .

△

Copyright @ 2024 by Diane A. Rose
All rights reserved.
Printed in the United States of America

ISBN: 9798339873754

Published by Diane A. Rose

Dewey Decimal Classification: 248.32.
Subject Heading: Religions / Christian Devotional Literature / Practical Theology / Christian Life / Experience and Practice / Prayer and Private Worship

Scripture quotations marked CSB have been taken from the Christian Standard Bible, Copyright 2017 by Holman Bible Publishers. Used by permission. Christian Standard Bible and CSB are federally registered
trademarks of Holman Bible Publishers.

Scripture quotations marked
NKJV have been taken
from the New King James Version,
Copyright @ 1985, 1983 by
Thomas Nelson, Inc.

*Dedicated to my awesome,
God-following husband,
Homer Price Rose!
Thank you for loving me as Christ
loves His Church.*

*Thank you, Homer, for always
setting an example of how to live
and sit before our Holy God,
Creator, Savior, and Lord,
Jesus Christ, the Messiah.*

Psalm 37:7
***Be silent before the Lord
and wait expectantly for Him.***

△

Contents

Chapter	Page
1 Places People in the Bible Prayed	8
2 Being Silent Before the Lord	14
3 Tools to Be Silent	23
4 Morning Prayer & Scripture Meditation	25
5 Journaling	29
6 Dream Journaling	34
7 Scripture Memorization	38
8 Silent Walks / Prayer Walks	42
9 Traffic Light Prayers	48
10 Sit in Silence While Driving	51
11 Prayer Garden	56
12 Prayerful Gardening	63
13 Water Front Prayers	61
14 Short Phrases	65

15 Listen to Christian Music
or Lyrics 68
16 Quote or Read Your
Favorite Verse 71
17 Sabbath Rest 73
18 Technology Fast / Technology
Sabbath 75
19 Unplugged Sabbath
Activities 78
20 Devotional Reading 80
21 Focus on God's Love
Focus on God's Work in
Your Life 82
22 Star Gazing 86
23 Shawl, Apron, Scarf —
Postures 88
24 Mindful Eating 91
25 Silent Dinner 95
26 Creative Expression 99
27 Prayerful Coloring 101
28 Gratitude Walk 103
29 Prayer Partnerships 107

30	Unplanned Moments	110
31	Holy Listening	114
32	Reflect on Your Day	117
33	Digital Sunset Ritual	119
34	What do I do next?	121

△

Places People in the Bible Prayed

Where does God's Word suggest we "sit before the Lord, in His Presence?"

Before we sit down seeking His face, let's mention a few of the places people have been known to pray, to be silent before the Lord. Notice the circumstances of each example.

Moses was on Mount Sinai. Exodus 34:28. He was there forty days and forty nights. He did not eat bread or drink water. He wrote, he journaled (author's emphasis). He wrote the Ten Commandments, the words of the covenant, on the tablets. People needed directions.

Do you ever need new directions?

Jonah prayed in the belly of the fish. Jonah 2:1-2. He was distressed and running from life. He was swallowed up by a fish. Do you ever feel like you are being swallowed up?

Nehemiah prayed in Susa. Nehemiah 1:4. He had heard that the walls of Jerusalem had fallen. The Israelites were in trouble and disgraced. He mourned for days and cried out to God for forgiveness and asked God specifically to listen to his prayer. He reminded God of all He had done for His people, Israel. Are you ever at the bottom of your strength to where you are aching for those around you? For your family? For your friends?

Hezekiah went to the Temple to pray. 2 Kings 19:14-15. His city was being threatened by the Assyrian army. He went to the Temple to pray when he received a threatening letter from the king of Assyria. God answered through the prophet Isaiah. When do you get threatened in your life? Do you go to a place of holiness to meet God? A place where you meet Him often, like at church, or worship?

Ezra was at the river side. Ezra 8:21. He was requesting safe travels for his family and all their possessions. God honored his prayer and fasting. Are you by a crossroads, a river you need to cross? Are you seeking God's provision in everything you are doing?

Daniel prayed at his window in his upper room. Daniel 6:10. Daniel received notice that people are to bow down to King Darius. He went into his house. With the windows in his upstairs room opened toward Jerusalem, three times a day he got down on his knees, prayed, and gave thanks to his God, just as he had done before. Do you go to your "upper room" and pray? Do you have a regular place to pray?

Paul and Silas prayed in prison. Acts 16:25. It was midnight. They were chained in their cell. They were praying and singing hymns to God, and the prisoners were listening to them. Do you feel like you are in prison? Do you want out? Are you praying and praising God for your situation?

Jesus prayed in the garden. Matthew 26:36.

He prayed on the Cross. Matthew 27:46.

He was about to face the hardest event any human would ever face, and He knew He needed His Father, God, to be able to face the next few days. He knew God was His answer for life's worst suffering—the dying on the Cross for all of mankind's sin. He was dying so we could again be in right relationship with our Creator.

You can always bring your concerns to God the Father through Jesus

Christ, His Son, for any circumstance you may be facing. Come and sit in silence in the Presence of the Father. He is waiting for His children to sit with Him. Those around you are watching you and what you say or do in difficult times as well as perfect times. Be His light and His hands.

△

Being Silent Before the Lord

Being silent before the Lord means coming home to the Father! It means sitting at His feet and soaking up all He has to say to me. It is being in my rightful place as the daughter of the Most High King. It is crawling up in "Daddy God's" lap, as one friend many years ago use to say.

I have great emotions when I think about "being home" with family. I was blessed to have an earthly Daddy, my Father, who let me crawl up in his lap. Though he went to heaven years ago, I remember the feeling of home and safety in his arms. When he would go places, many times I'd get to go, too. (I learned as an adult that my hyper-personality was sometimes overwhelming to my Mother, so Daddy "helped" her out by taking me on excursions with him.) That warmth, safe, presence that I always remember with my Father is what I find when I'm silent before the Lord now. My loving husband creates a welcoming space for our children, grandchildren, and great-grandchildren. It is "OK" to just sit and enjoy being in each other's presence in the house.

When was the last time you sat in silence, truly quiet, and allowed your soul to breathe? Allowed your heart to be quiet? Allowed the world around you with all of its own demands to be ignored and you just enjoyed the presence of some silence?

Have you found that sweet spot in your daily schedule? I really enjoy the moments of silence, resting in the Lord when the day is so full. I'm known for taking a full lunch hour. Many times this is just to get away from the intense commitment I have to my work, to pause during the day to visit with a friend, make new friends or just wait on the Lord in the silence of the moment.

Another way to say this is, *Are you listening to your "First Love"?* Do you know the Lord, Jehovah, through Jesus Christ, as your First Love?

I remember well the first time a pastor friend asked me, this question: Who is your first love? I wasn't really sure what He meant. But I could tell that even if it was to be a fresh, new idea to me at the moment, I needed to embrace whatever this pastor was going to tell me.

I found myself returning to the home I grew up in with three children, ages twelve, five, and nine days old. We arrived via airplane on Friday afternoon. We went to church on Sunday. I knew I needed some support and help to get me through my situation. I asked a retired pastor I knew from years ago if I could talk with him. We met in the church parlor, a nice comfortable living-room style place with some privacy. He asked me: Who is your "first love"? He guided me to the moment when I first asked Jesus into my life at the age of seven years old. What did I believe? I believed that all of us have done wrong, Romans 3:23. I believed in Jesus and believed He would save me, Acts 16:31. Then if I confessed with my mouth that "Jesus is Lord" and if I believed God raised Him from the dead, I'd be saved, Romans 10:9-10. These were the steps I took to ask Jesus to become my "First Love"! He did come to live in my heart. Jesus has never left me. This pastor reminded me that my "First Love" is the One that created me and gave me a choice to spend time with Him.

To deal with my newest situation, I needed to first remember that I belong to Jesus because He chose me and I said, Yes!   Starting back at those emotions and facts about my personal salvation in those difficult times allowed me to get a fresh, new start in my life. The bumps in the road would not be easy to maneuver, but I could go over them, go around them, or go through them with the guidance my Jesus wants to give me every day.

In the hustle and bustle of our daily lives, we often forget the time that God wants to spend with us. God wants to sit at the table with your cup of coffee (or tea in my case) and interact with you as your Father and you as His child.

The simple beauty of stillness—quiet—is ready for the choosing when we look to our "First Love" for His Presence. As I began to spend moments of quiet with God, I began to move ahead in life even with the circumstances that I found myself in during those rough years.

Psalm 37:7 reminds us to **"Be silent before the Lord and wait expectantly for Him."** (CSB) This is a profound invitation to step away from the noise and find rest in the Presence of God.

Prioritize your relationship with God and you can find ways to incorporate and cultivate stillness in your daily walk as you accept His invitation to "be silent before the Lord."

Be aware that some of your silence may invoke the need for you to speak to God for a moment or say a prayer aloud to get started.

Some places will find you, not in a private setting, but with your posture, your attitude, and your position separating you from those around you so you can hear God's voice speaking to you through the Holy Spirit, within your own spirit.

Some words will be said within your heart and mind and not aloud. Do not limit yourself to having your lips be still. Speak from your heart even in the whisper of your mind.

How you speak into the silence can be as unique as you are.

△

Tools to Be Silent

In the next few pages, you will find practical ways you can begin to create space in your life that welcomes the still, small voice of the Father (1 Kings 19:11-13 CSB): *Then He said, "Go out and stand on the mountain in the Lord's presence." At that moment, the Lord passed by. A great and mighty wind was tearing at the mountains and was shattering cliffs before the Lord, but the Lord was not in the wind. After the wind there was an earthquake, but the Lord was not in the earthquake. After the earthquake there was a fire, but the Lord was not in the fire. And after the fire there was a voice, a soft whisper. When Elijah heard it, he wrapped his face in his mantle and went out and stood at the entrance of the cave.*

Read through each one of the tools and try one for a few days or a week. Then add another throughout the day or just try another for another week. You will find that as you try each one, they will fit into your life at different moments, at different circumstances.

Let God lead YOU as you reach out to Him for His Presence to fill each moment of every day!

△

Morning Prayer & Scripture Meditation

Before the world shows up in your life, give God your day by spending time with Him. Start by praying something like this before you even get out of bed: Lord, thank you for a new day. This is Your day which You have made just for me and I can rejoice and be glad in it. (Author's paraphrase of Psalm 118:24)

Don't rush this time. Jesus wants to spend time with you.   He wants to hear you read His Words—the Scriptures—the Bible. He wants to share something with you that will make your day the best it can be. Your time with Him will make the rest of your day flow so much better than you can imagine.

    Remember He IS the Creator of the world. He can create great days beyond our imaginations! Your expectations for the day will be focused on Him and His Words. He must be the priority in your life, and He will be as you spend time just with Him.

    Pray first. Ask the Holy Spirit who lives within you as a believer to open your spiritual eyes and ears to hear and see what God is wanting to say to you at this particular moment. Use your Bible and a blank journal to write down what God is saying. The verses where you start are not as important as just starting. Begin to hear what

God is saying by opening His Word and reading. You might start with the Psalms, or Proverbs, or the Gospel of John, or 1 John.

As you "hear" Him speak through the Words on the pages of the Bible (or on your phone app) you can know His Presence wherever you find yourself. Having a hard copy of the Word, the Bible, to hold in your hands allows you to use your sense of touch to "hear" His Words right from the pages in front of you. Personally, I like to highlight, with a marker made for delicate pages, the words that "jump off the page" for me during the time I'm reading. Sometimes it is a complete verse or it may be only a phrase or a few words.

Note:

I remember Jack Taylor, a pastor in Texas, talking about the "battle of the blankets" years ago when I heard him speak. Every morning as he was trying to get out of bed, there would be this fight with his blankets. Do I get up or not? Do I cover my shoulders back up or get up? Can I have just a few more moments in bed, Lord? He fought the blankets regularly. He learned through the years he had to get up, shower, and dress for the brand new day first. Then he would get his Bible and journal and sit down with his cup of coffee and be with his heavenly Father. He fought this "battle of the blankets," but God won out when he got himself awake and ready to listen to what God had in store for him on any given day.

△

Journaling

Journaling: Pour out your thoughts, prayers, and reflections in a journal. Create a space for honesty between you and God— between you and Your Heavenly Father.

Sometimes these thoughts come from your Bible reading. Sometimes you might read an inspirational phrase or poem or story. Journaling allows your mind to "empty" onto the paper. As you make room in your head for God's voice, your hands are helping you put the thoughts on paper.

What am I writing? You are pausing in your quiet, still moment to listen to your Father as He speaks. After reading a passage of Scripture, ask yourself, what is God saying to me at this moment? How do these thoughts relate to what I know these verses are saying to do? What actions do I need to take right now to be obedient to this message?

The more senses you use during this time the more you will learn from the experience. For example: Use the five senses: hearing, sight, smell, taste, and touch. In the journaling process you "hear" when reading aloud a passage, the printed word. Also, as you let God talk to you, you can "hear" His voice in the stillness. You "see" by using your eyes to read it. One way to use the sense of "smell" is if you have smells around you that remind you of the passage you are reading. If I am in nature and I smell the fresh cut grass around me, I might relate that smell to the words I am hearing and seeing. You might use a fragrance from a candle or lotion every time you pause to write in your journal.

Intentionally create a special fragrance around you as you journal so you can relate those words and experience, to that smell as you are out and about during the day.

Having your journal with you in your bag or purse can offer you opportunities to put things down on paper when you hear or see them throughout the day. I heard someone say years ago, the faintest ink is worth the best memory. So write it down when it comes to your attention. I've found at times, I can say the quote into my personal text message to myself on my phone when I can't write it down immediately.

One blessing to journaling is being able to take time to reflect periodically on what you have written. Every three to six months, take an extended time to go back and re-read what you have written. What is the theme, the pattern, you see in all these passages? What has God been trying to tell you in your journaling? What have you yet to act upon?

For me, I'm a bit slow when it comes to learning something new at times. I have to hear it again and again before I realize He's talking to me, not my neighbor or another family member. I am the one God is molding and I have a responsibility as His child to stop and listen to what He is saying and apply it to my life. Journaling can help you clear your mind. It allows you to actually see in your own handwriting what God is saying to you.

Dream Journaling

Dream Journaling: Be prepared to record dreams and reflections when you wake up. Keep a journal by your bedside and recognize that God often speaks to us through our dreams or through the quiet moments of rest. Or keep a small pad in your bathroom so you can write items down when you wake up during the night.

At times I may be getting up from a nap or just laying my body down to take a break and get off my feet. God will say something through the Holy Spirit and I want to be sure I remember it. I'll write it on something by my bed. Or I'll pick up my phone and write it on a text to myself. *(It is dangerous for me to pick up my phone at anytime because I have a tendency to "check other things" when it is in my hand!! So know yourself!!)* Use a pad of paper or small note book. You can get small pads at a discount store, dollar store, to have them lying around on end tables, by your bedside, in the bathroom, or in your purse. Then combine them into your regular journal before heading off to bed at night as you thank God for speaking to you throughout the day.

    Recognize, too, that when you put your head on your pillow, it may be one of the first times during the day that you have stopped. God can speak to us during the night because we are finally quiet enough to listen.

Another part of "dream journaling" is to not hold back on any dreams you may have while you are awake and planning for the future. What do you hear God telling you about? What is He letting you see around you? What desires has He put in your heart as you are out and about in your daily walk?

Take time to write down anything you sense God is talking to you about. What keeps coming up around you in conversations? What do you keep hearing during a sermon or message?

Write out Scriptures He is showing you as you walk, or run, through your day. When you review your journaling in the months ahead, you will become aware that there is a theme in what God has been telling you. He has a specific task just for you. He will tell you as you spend time with Him in the quiet stillness of your life and as you record what He has been putting on your heart. These dreams can come true as they measure up to His plan in your life.

△

Scripture Memorization

Scripture Memorization: Use God's own Words to pray back to Him. Commit Scripture verses to memory and allow God's Word to dwell richly in your heart and guide your thoughts and actions throughout the day.

Choose a passage such as Psalm 37:7
Be silent before the Lord and wait expectantly for Him.
Psalm 37:7

Always say the address of the verse first and after you've said the verse, as you are memorizing it. If at any time you can't remember all the words, you will have a better chance at remembering where it is found in the Scriptures.

Start by saying the book, chapter, and verse. Then say the first phrase of the verse: *Psalm 37:7, Be silent before the Lord*.

Do this several times a day. When you get up in the morning, while you are brushing your teeth, as you shower, while you are putting on your clothes, and before you leave your home for the day's work are a few times you might consider.

Write the passage on index cards and put it in your car, or in your briefcase or in your purse so you will come across it during your day. Put it on a sticky note on your dashboard.

Allow you mind to hold onto this phrase. After seven days of memorizing this phrase, add more of the verse to your memorizing. *Psalm 37:7 Be silent before the Lord and wait expectantly for Him. Psalm 37:7*

Now you are ready to work on the verse for the next week using both phrases. Habits are developed through repetition. So keep repeating until the verse is "yours"—no one can take away what you have memorized. Hold true to God's Words in your heart.

Go a step further with this memorization and begin to add a

new verse to memorize every third week. In six months you will have memorized nine new verses that can give you moments of silence in Him for the rest of your life.

    Putting God's Word in your heart is life changing! Psalm 119:11 *I have treasured your word in my heart so that I may not sin against you.* CSB

△

Silent Walks / Prayer Walks

Silent Walks / Prayer Walks: Take a leisurely walk around the neighborhood. Walk through the local park. Take a mid-day break and walk around the office parking lot. Drive to a local mall or shopping center, get out and just walk around. Take a hike on a local trail. Do these different walks in silence just listening for His still, small voice. Intentionally intercede for the people and places you encounter along the way.

Intentionally head out to walk silently. Ask God to show you what He wants you to see today as you walk. If you are concerned about your time and only have a limited segment to give to this walk, set an alarm on your phone or watch so you can concentrate on listening to God and not be worried, "Is my time up?"

Pray for people you see in your walk. They don't need to know you are praying. This is a conversation between you and God. You are walking to be in tune with Him. As your thoughts wander, give those thoughts back to God. Keep watching with expectancy for what He wants you to see on this day and in this physical space in your life.

Places you might consider to do prayer walks could include your local church yard, the place you meet to worship, your street in your neighborhood, the local schools whether they be elementary, middle school, academies, high schools—upper grades, and businesses you want to thrive in your community.

    Pray for safety within the walls of these establishments. Pray for the people who will be coming and going. Pray for God's Spirit to fill the churches so people can know who He is. Pray for the message to be preached to be centered, targeted, specifically for those who need a true Word from Jesus today. Pray for each to hear the Word given for them. Pray for healing in the lives of those who come to worship. It could be physical, emotional, psychological, mental healings. Pray for the attitudes of the people to be centered in God's love toward everyone. (Jesus did come for everyone, that none would be lost. Luke 19:10 *For the Son of Man has come to seek and to save the lost.* CSB) Pray for the children's workers to love the children as Jesus loves them. Pray for the simplicity of the gospel message to be given for these children who come to the church yard.

    Pray for the neighbors as you walk who you may not even know. Pray for whoever lives in the houses around you. Pray for kids to enjoy the blessings of the homes they live in. Pray for peace and security and safety for all the people living in each house. Pray for relationships to be God-honoring. Pray for learning and family worship times for each home. Pray by name for those you know their names. Pray for job opportunities for your neighbors to thrive in your community. Pray for the businesses they run to be honorable in all their endeavors. Pray for financial needs, physical needs, emotional needs, and whatever God brings to mind as you walk by a neighbor. Speak, greet, and smile at those you meet as you go.

Pray for safety in the schools. Pray for each child, teacher, administrator in each school. Pray for those you know personally by name. Pray for them to become leaders who live by biblical truths within their school communities. Pray for the words and attitudes within the classrooms to be God-honoring and God-loving toward each individual. Pray for those you may know who are struggling. Pray for mentors to come along side students who need extra support. Pray for volunteers to provide needed supplies to those less fortunate. Pray for God to raise up individuals who can have a voice for those who are not able to share their personal needs. Pray for learning atmospheres where every child can become all they are created to be.

   As you walk, pray for God to show you where He wants you to become more involved in His work around you. Pray you can and will be all that He created you to become.

△

Traffic Light Prayers

Traffic Light Prayers: SMILE with me! I know you smiled as you read that title!!   Look in your rearview mirror. Ask God to bless the driver in the vehicle behind you. If there is an "intense conversation" going on, I usually say, "Lord, zap them! Stop them and let them know YOU are Present!" If it seems to be a couple, pray for their marriage.   If it is a parent-child type of situation, pray for clarity of understanding and pouring out of love between the two. Look at the people around you and ask God to allow you to share a smile with them. Then smile!

One of my favorite sayings from Henry Blackaby's

<u>Experiencing God: Knowing & Doing the Will of God</u> Bible study is "God is at work around us. We need to join him."

When you are in your car you can choose to have silent moments with God. One way is to lift up prayers for those people you see around you. Pray for people in the cars behind you. Pray for those in the cars beside you. If they see you looking at them, smile really big! Make them think you know something they don't know. You do! You just prayed for them.

Stopping at the traffic light and praying for those around you keeps your focus on God and what He is doing in the lives of those around you. You may never know this side of heaven how effective your prayers were, but you can continue to pray for people wherever they cross your paths.

A friend shared with me that when she read about the traffic light prayers, it reminded her of a time when she went through a local drive-thru. "I looked in my rearview mirror and the lady behind me looked like she was going through a hard time. I watched her while I waited. When I got to the window, I paid for her meal. I prayed that it would let her know God cared about her." This is a good example of being aware of your surroundings, aware of the Presence of the Lord, and aware of what you can do as the hands for the Father in helping another person.

△

Sit in Silence While Driving

Sit in Silence While Driving:
This is intentionally being in your car in silence. Before you start the car or as you are driving and realize you can be silent for these moments, say a prayer something like this: *Lord, I want to sit here in silence to hear Your Words in my heart and mind. Thank you for joining me in this moment.*

As you are driving, God will bring to your mind people He wants you to intercede for, people you need to be praying for at that moment. I see a "blue car" and I think of my three children who all have a family joke about a "blue car." I smile and pray for those in the "blue car" and for my children.

You might see a neighbor or a neighbor's place and God says to pray for them. When you join Him in the intercession, you are drawn into His Presence.

You pass a school and begin praying for school kids, teachers, sports teams, band and orchestra groups. You pray for the principal to be God-fearing, loving to every child under his care.

You pass the grocery store and thank God for his provisions. You pray for those who are less fortunate and ask God to provide for them as they are trying to decide what they have money to buy and making it stretch as far as it can go. You thank God for the farmers who sowed the seeds and tiled the ground just so you could have food in your favorite grocery store. You thank God for the truckers and train engineers who make the trek across the country on the highways and byways to get the food closer to you. You thank God for the highways that make it so much easier to travel today than just a few years ago.

You slow down for emergency equipment on its way to some emergency because their lights and sirens are going strong. You pray for the people involved to not be hurt and to be safe in whatever the situation is during this emergency. You pray for wisdom for the EMTs (ambulance personnel) and firefighters as they approach the situation. You pray for those around the folks to move out to the way for the professionals to be able to reach those in need. You pray for the ambulance folks to get their patients to the hospital in a timely manner for the best care possible. You thank God that you can lift up these strangers to Him and realize God knows each one of them Himself. You ask God to touch their lives at their point of need in all areas of life: physical, emotional, psychological, financial, and spiritual.

△

Prayer Garden

Prayer Garden: Find a serene spot in nature—a park, garden, or forest. Spend time soaking in the beauty of God's creation.

Any garden or natural outdoor setting can become your prayer garden—a place of prayer in the middle of God's beautiful creation. There are several national park areas in my community. Go walk a trail and stop on one of the benches and pray.

Create a spot in your own yard where there may be bushes or flower beds or small trees separating an area for you to put a bench for you and a bench for Jesus to sit on. A favorite spot of one of my missionary friends was her prayer garden in her back yard. She had a few stones piled in the middle with two benches around the stones. These stones reminded her of the many alters built by people in the Old Testament who were reminded that their stones were placed where they met God. She told me the benches were a physical reminder that God was sitting with her in her silence, in her time of fellowship, and in her time of need.

 Find a spot in a garden, a public garden will work, and sit in silence remembering who God is in your life. There may be a public park near you that has a garden-style walk way. Use this to walk and listen in silence for God's

Presence. A local mountain trail where you can walk around the base of the mountain or trek up the hill for a bit. Sit awhile in nature.

I'm reminded by a family member that one of our Daddy's favorite hymns was "In the Garden,"

Here are the words to jog your memory if you remember the song or to introduce you to the words if it is "new" to you:

I come to the garden alone,
While to dew is still on the roses;
And the voice I hear, falling on my ear,
The Son of God discloses.

And He walks with me,
And He talks with me,
And He tells me I am His own,

*And the joy we share
As we tarry there,
None other has ever known.*

*He speaks, and the sound of His voice,
Is so sweet the birds hush their singing;
And the melody that He gave to me
Within my heart is ringing.*

*And He walks with me,
And He talks with me,
And He tells me I am His own,
And the joy we share
As we tarry there,
None other has ever known.*

*I'd stay in the garden with Him
Tho' the night around me be falling;
But He bids me go;
through the voice of woe,
His voice to me is calling.*

And He walks with me,
And He talks with me,
And He tells me I am His own,
And the joy we share
As we tarry there,
None other has ever known.

C. Austin Miles, 1912.
Public Domain.

△

Prayerful Gardening

Prayerful Gardening: Spend time tending to a garden, or houseplants, using the act of gardening as a form of prayer and communion with God's creation.

Example: Homer loved his garden. He had one for years until his strength would not carry him to the back of our lot. I loved coming home or heading out to speak to him when I was overcome with the sweet voice of song as he sang praises to His Heavenly Father. He was singing at the top of his lungs and they—God and Homer—were all that mattered! What a blessing I have had so many times just being reminded of God's grace in my life when He brought Homer and me together. God always blessed Homer's faithfulness to Him and the garden always provided great sustenance to us throughout the spring, summer and even into the fall!

If you are a gardener, or a gardener want-to-be, try something small and let it grow, literally grow, into a special place of prayer. During the years I lived in Texas, we joined a community project where each family was to plant a 4 foot by 6 foot garden spot. Plant what you liked and then share your bounty with your neighbors. Even with my "brown thumb" it was a special time for the months we had this garden.

△

Water Front Prayers

Water Front Prayers: Stretch out on a beach towel at the beach. Walk the beach with your feet in the water's edge. (Remember the water magnifies the sun rays and can sunburn the top of your feet—be aware! Speaking from experience!)

Listen to the sound of the water. The waves lapping up on the shore in rhythm make "music" as you hear the water move. Hear the joyful voices of people around you enjoy family time in the water. Thank God for this place to see the majesty of His creation, the ocean, the sand, the lake, the water, and the creatures of the sea.

Take a canoe on the river and enjoy God's creation all around you. Sit quietly in the water as the current moves you along. Mediate on God's Presence around you. Notice the water current changes as the terrain changes on the sides of the river or with rocks or small islands jutting up from the river basin.

Bask in the sunshine. Soak up the warm breeze. Recognize God made all creation for us to enjoy. Pray for those around you to enjoy this time outside with you. Thank God for the presence of others with you. Appreciate all that God has done in your life to bring you to this place at this moment in time.

△

Short Phrases

Short Phrases:
   God of Mercy
   God, my Father
   Jesus, Son of God
   Praise Your Name, Jesus!
   I love you, Lord!

Pick a familiar phrase from the Word, from the Psalms, or a portion of a favorite verse. Say it aloud or in your heart. Repeat it slowly. Pause. Think about what it says. What does it mean to you? Give Praise to God as you speak the phrase. Pause. Listen to what God is saying to you in your heart and mind. Repeat the phrase again. Pause. Listen.

During one of the rough times in my life, I had a counselor to tell me to stop trying to read so much of the Bible (a chapter or two) in one sitting. You just need to pause. Read one phrase: *God is love.* Find pictures that remind you of His love. Carry those pictures with you (today we have phones where we can store pictures and phrases) so you can embrace the joy it brings with the phrase. Nature offers so many beautiful picturesque opportunities. Find the picture you love, then find the phrase in His Word that meets you today where you are in your walk with Him. Put them together.

There are many sources in our technological world that have "phrases" with pictures.

NOTE: Not all phrases are biblically based. Satan just changed one word in his message to Eve in the Garden of Eden. Do not be tempted by "great phrases". Be sure you are keeping those that are Scriptures and share sound biblical truths.

    Fill your life with truth. Pause and enjoy each word in His Presence as you quote them back to Him. Share them with your heavenly Father and thank Him for what the words and phrases mean to you in the moment.

△

Listen to Christin Music or Lyrics

Listen to Christian Music or Lyrics: With music options in your hand, you can listen to your favorite Christian music almost anywhere you go. Choose playlists that have Different themes in Christian music…praise, worship, hymns, God's presence, Christian rock, Southern Gospel, and your own selection of favorites.

Sometimes you may want certain music for specific times of the day: morning commute or sitting in rush hour or on the way home from work or relaxing in the evening, or just a moment of quiet.

Prepare in advance for these moments by creating the playlists that fit your personal needs. When you hear a song you like on the radio (cars still have radios and several great Christian radio stations are out there), make a note—speak it into your text messages to yourself. When the choir or worship team at church sings something that touches your heart, make a note. Find the song. Listen to it again. Check out the lyrics on the Internet and hear the words that were making an impact in your life.

Make time for a "date night" with a Christian concert. Plan ahead for a family trip to hear one of your favorite artists. Check out local concerts and see if a Christian artist is playing in your town. Take a friend to enjoy the music with you and be sure to get a copy of your favorite songs. You will want to listen again and again after being there.

△

Quote or Read Your Favorite Verse

Quote or read your favorite verse: Carry verses in your heart (Scripture memorization mentioned earlier). Create a note on your phone with your favorite verses. Make cards with verses you are studying in your current Bible study. Write your favorite verses on the inside cover of your journal.

Use these verses to read as you sit and enjoy the Presence of God at any moment in time. Reflect on the meaning. Remember what made it a "favorite."

How has God used this verse in your life already? How does the verse relate to your current situation? Is God telling you something new or re-emphasizing what He is doing in your life right now?

Share your favorite verse you've reviewed today with someone who is growing alongside you in your personal walk.

△

Sabbath Rest

Sabbath Rest — Set aside a full day for Sabbath rest, refraining from work and embracing in relaxing and Refreshing activities that nourish your soul. (If you are serving or working on Sundays, then set aside another day like Monday or Saturday to be your Sabbath Rest.) Exodus 20:8-11

    Choose activities that bring your focus back to God and His character and His presence in your life.

    God told His people, Israel, to work six days and take the seventh day as a Sabbath. Our bodies and mind and spirit all need a rest, a break each week. Taking a day for worship, praise, and family is a great way to celebrate God in our lives regularly.

Establish time in your schedule to have Sabbath rest where you allow yourself to create. To find margin—time away from the going and going and going—where you can hear God speaking and allow Him to create newness in your life and daily walk with Him.

Note: I recommend the Bible Study
Breathe: Making Room for Sabbath by
Priscilla Shirer as a great place to find your Sabbath. She gives practical ways to make room to breathe in your every day activities. *Published by Adult Ministry Publishing. LifeWay Press. LifeWay Church Resources. One LifeWay Plaza, Nashville TN 37234-0113. 2014 by Pricilla Shirer. www.lifeway.com*

△

Technology Fast / Technology Sabbath

Technology Fast - Take a break from the screens and distractions allowing yourself to disconnect and be fully present with God and yourself.

Or Technology Sabbath - Designate a day each week to unplug completely from technology, allowing yourself to fully rest and be present with God and loved ones. Spending time with other believers in corporate worship and sharing what God has done in your life this past week makes a Sabbath, a Sunday, extra special.

Another alternative to this might be a ***Digital Detox Retreat*** - Plan a weekend retreat in a place without internet or cell service, immersing yourself in nature and disconnecting from the distractions of technology. Sit in silence in the moments you might have used your technology, but this time reflect on the quiet whisper of the voice of God.

You might take breaks at different times during the day. Carve out places to rest in the Presence of the Lord. In the past you might have picked up your cell phone and checked emails or strolled through reels. Choose to take a break periodically during the day and pause for this moment of reflection and conversation with your heavenly Father.

△

Unplugged Sabbath Activities

Unplugged Sabbath Activities:
Plan Sabbath activities that do not require electricity or screens, such as board games, hiking or picnicking in nature. Mexican Train is a favorite for my family. Singing around the keyboard or piano can make the day extra special as you sing old hymn favorites or choruses that bring back great memories of God's Presence in your lives.

Schedule time to just have conversations with family and friends. Don't rush through your meal. My husband says, "No watch; it is a social time." We are not to be influenced by a time to go, just by the opportunity to be together and listen to what is happening with each other.

   Let spontaneous responses be the norm for the day. Do what naturally falls into place for the group of folks around you.   Listen for God's creativity in your life. Respond to what He is doing around you as you learn to unplug from the routines of your six work days.

△

Devotional Reading

Devotional Reading: Read your devotion in a slow, savoring fashion and reflect on what you are reading.

Choose a devotional book by an author you enjoy. You might use one that is done by the calendar date, January 1, January 2, etc. If you use one of these, make a note in the top corner of the page you are reading with the current year. This way you can know how many times you have gone through the book or you may notice you have seasons during the year that you use the book more often than at other times.

There are several great writers who have daily devotions on

Instagram or emails subscriptions. If you are currently in a Bible study group, you might use that material for your devotional guide.

Bite off small bits of information. Don't try to read too much. Just let the article soak into your mind, your heart and your soul. Ask God to open your eyes and spiritual ears to hear what is being said in the reading. Then reflect on God's voice in your heart. Make notes so you can remember what God has been doing in your devotional times in the past days and weeks and months.

△

Focus on God's Love Focus on God's Work in Your Life

Sit and Focus on God's Love:
Focus on the verses you know or the experiences where you have personally seen God's love in your life. Focus on where God is working currently in your life to love one another.

God is Love. 1 John 4:8; John 3:16

How has God showed His love to you personally? Yes, He died for you and He rose again and lives today for you! Make a list of mile markers in your life. What are significant places where you remember God's love showing up in your life? Your salvation experience might be the first one. Or it might be people or places you can look back on in your life where God was there and working and you didn't know it at the time. Make notes of what you are remembering. It might be a summer camp experience or a college retreat. Maybe you remember God's love when He introduced you to your spouse, the love of your life. Could be you remember God's hand in an accident or tragedy where He showed up through friends and family when you needed it most. Mark these memories and see how much God has done for you.

Now list all the ways you see God working in your life today! How did you get where you are?

Reflect on how you got there. Did you see God along the way? Or did you forget He was there and are struggling now? Remember where He has been and what He has done. Look for ways to remember the great moments and times you were closest to God. Can you see a pattern in your life? Do you need to go back to the last moment you remember Him working in your life and start again? What were you doing to keep His love in the forefront of your existence? Where do you need to go in your relationship with Him so you can see God's love right now? What does God seem to be showing you about your current work situation or life circumstances?

God is Love.   He is loving you. He wants you to know He loves you more than you can imagine.

Focus on His love. His gift of Jesus. His presence for every place you find yourself, even right now.

△

Star Gazing

Star Gazing: Spend time under the stars, remembering the vastness of God's creation and the wonder of His presence in the universe.

Set your lawn chairs out on the patio at sunset. As the stars begin to come into view, bask in the beauty of the sky. Start counting the stars. Too many to count? Yes! God in His creation put so many stars in place that we can count all our lives and still not get to all of them! The pure vastness of the heavens can draw us silently to His Presence. Relax in your chair and notice the patterns in the stars. We are in the Milky Way galaxy, just one of many God created. He knows the stars by name. (Isaiah 40:26 *He brings out the starry host by number; He calls all of them by name. Because of His great power and strength, not one of them is missing.)*

In the city lights it is hard to see the stars at night. Find a spot that works for you to gaze at the stars. You might even find a planetarium in your community to sit and see the stars. If you can't see the stars in your community, make the effort to vacation or pause in your work to find a place in a nearby community to just watch the stars.

△

Shawl, Apron, Scarf — Postures

Shawl, Apron, Scarf — Postures: clothing items can say to those around you, "I'm praying. Please don't bother me right now." How you present yourself to the Lord is important. When you physically separate yourself from the world around you with the shawl or apron or scarf, you are telling yourself, your mindset, you are ready for your meeting with the Lord.

Sometimes in our busy days, hectic schedules, we need to have a way to set ourselves apart from the people and duties around us. Putting a particular shawl over your head or an apron around your waist can let others know you are praying. While you're cooking a meal or cleaning up after a meal, intentionally set yourself apart to focus on Jesus and His provision in your life while doing those tasks. My Mother had "her chair" in her bedroom where she sat. I could find her there when I got home from school. It was "her place." Her posture was a readiness for God to speak.

The particular item of clothing doesn't matter, it is just the act of intentionally setting yourself aside and letting your own mental state know, I'm going to pray and praise and focus on my heavenly Father while I'm in this moment. If your home is full of people all the time, this may be a way to say, "Mommy is busy at the moment. Come back in a little bit."

    During a worship service or gathering, you might choose to wear a scarf over your head to, again, focus more intently on the Father and His conversation with you personally.

△

Mindful Eating

Mindful Eating: Slow down. Say your blessing for the food before you with reverence and respect for the Creator, Jehovah Jirah, my Provider. Express gratitude for God's provision to nurture your body as a temple of the Holy Spirit.

Thank God for the taste. Thank God for the taste buds He gave you to enjoy the variety of flavors in front of you at the table. Let's say, for example, you are eating a salad with pieces of chicken on top. Thank you for the lettuce and the fresh green color that makes it pleasing to the eye. Thank God for the garden where the lettuce and cucumber were grown. Thank God for the tomatoes, the farmer who raised them, the sunshine and rain which was needed to help them grow. Thank God for the chickens. Thank God for the guys who built the chicken houses and the coops, for the farmers to raise the chickens in abundance so you could just enjoy them at this moment. (I had a family member who was once on a crew that built chicken houses. They started at 4 AM and worked long hours to make them ready for the chickens.) Thank God for the spices on the chicken that bring out the rich flavor. Thank God for the cheese and the cow who gave the fresh milk to make the cheese. Thank God for the plate and utensils you are using to eat your meal. Thank God for the napkin, the paper mill where the paper was made from a tree before it was ever put on your table.

Oh, isn't this fun!?! What a special way to be grateful intentionally for what is set before YOU! This could be a fun, regular event at your table for family and friends and guests. Let the children, and adults, learn where their food actually came from to get to you. All good things come from the Father above by way of so many other people! We are not "on an island" when it comes to meeting our daily needs. Listen in your silence as God reminds of His provision.

When you are eating out, be mindful of the staff in the restaurant. Pray for the cook, the chef, the servers, the owners, and the proprietors. Pray for the food to be pleasing to your eye as well as you palate.

    I have built relationships through the years eating at the same establishments for lunch. Many times I ask the server, "What can I pray for you about?" It opens up conversations that only God could orchestrate.

    Listen to the voice of the Father as you sit and eat and share words with those serving your food. Being mindful of your surroundings is as important as the food you are eating.

△

Silent Dinner

Silent Dinner: Perhaps you have a couple in your life or a few very close friends that you can invite to come for this special time of prayer and appreciation. The simple act of eating together becomes a sacred experience as you enjoy the presence of each other and enjoy the presence of God in your lives as brothers and sisters in Christ.

Folks that know me would say they'd come to a silent dinner just to see if I could be silent! Thank you, friends. But this is an opportunity to set aside dedicated time to pray with friends. You are nourishing your soul with intimacy with the heavenly Father as you nourish your body with great food and tastes.

    Start by setting the stage for this time. Soft instrumental music of your favorite hymns can be playing in the background. After greeting everyone, you can lead them to the table. Have place settings with a small note pad and pen for writing down prayer requests as they come to mind. Have a blessing for the food and the time we are together. Encourage each one to savor the food. Look around the table and pray in your heart for each person. Pray for their unspoken requests and for God to reach down and touch them in ways only God can do. Pray for the food to taste extra favorable in honor of God's Presence in the room.

    After serving dessert, pray aloud to end the meal. Ask for God's blessing on each person and that they will leave as a changed person because they have been in the Presence of our Almighty Father who loves each of us more than we can ever imagine.

    As the hostess, send a handwritten note to each person who came to this silent dinner. Thank them for setting aside time to pray with you and the others. Thank them for being in your life. Remind them that you have prayed for them.   After you sign the card, stop. Yes, stop right then and there and pray for them.   Be true to what you said you would do. Pray for them. Continue to pray for them as they come to mind. Praying without ceasing is real. (1 Thessalonians 5:17 *Pray constantly. CSB)* Be in the attitude of prayer all day long so when one of the dinner friends comes to mind, you will pray!

△

Creative Expression

Creative Expression - Engage in a creative activity such as painting, drawing or writing poetry as a form of prayer and worship.

Begin with a blank sheet of paper and some colored pencils or pens.
- ✓ Sit quietly and listen for God's Presence.
- ✓ Read a word, a verse, a passage from the Scriptures, Bible. (Try Psalm 37:7 — *Be silent before the Lord, wait expectantly for Him.*)
- ✓ Doodle as you did perhaps when you were younger. Make circles or triangles or squares or dots.

- ✔ Do a few scribbles. Make lines.
- ✔ Connect the dots.

Listen for God to remind you of the needs around you. Who does He bring to mind? Write those names on the paper.

Add color to the page.

Add a phrase, or write a poem. Write a poem you are remembering as you pray.

Prayerful Coloring

Prayerful Coloring: Engage in coloring books with designs inspired by Scriptures, using the activity as a form of prayer and meditation.

Place a bag of scripture cards or scripture coloring books in a bag with colored pencils or pens near your favorite chair or by the living room couch. Take a few moments to just color and reflect on the words you are seeing on the page as you color.

Set aside a time each month just to color. A friend in the past used to say to me, "Coloring is the best stress reliever." That has been true many times when I've stopped to just color in the lines on a page from one of these coloring books.

△

Gratitude Walk

Gratitude Walk - Take a walk outdoors and intentionally notice the blessings around you, expressing gratitude to God for His goodness and provision. Neighborhood walks or a nature trail near by….

    As you take a walk, whether it is in the early morning, late afternoon, or evening, go with the intention of being grateful for all you have been given.   You can start from you feet and move up. Thank you, God, for my shoes to cover my feet. Thank you, God that I have feet with which to walk that are healthy and strong and will hold me up. Thank you for the socks, compression socks for some people, that help to keep the circulation going during the day. Thank you, Lord, for my legs, both of my legs that move when I want to move and stop when I asked them to stop. Thank you for the clothes I have to cover my body and protect me from the elements of wind and rain and sun. I'm grateful for my arms to hug my family, to hold my books, to carry my children and now my grandchildren. I'm grateful for my body that holds a healthy heart, breathing lungs, blood and blood veins that circulate life through every part of the body. I'm thankful, grateful, for my head with eyes to see, ears to hear, nose to smell, mouth to taste and mouth to speak. Thank you, Lord, for the brain you gave me as the command station for my body's activities.

Thank you, God, for the brain that continues to learn new things every day. Thank you that there are no limits to the expansion of my knowledge. Thank you, Lord, that my body is the place Your Holy Spirit can reside to guide me through each and every day.

    Re-focus and be grateful for your work, your neighbors, the new people you will meet today, the great food you will eat, and the silent moments God will give you to pause and just be in His Presence. Be grateful for your clients, your employees, your employer, you place of work that is comfortable and accessible to your personal needs. Be grateful for the verses you read this morning that keep showing up as you go through the day from radio messages, podcasts, instagram photos, and songs you hear from your playlist or scrolling through YouTube or Pandora. Be thankful God keeps bringing you back to His message just for you as you are grateful.

    Be grateful. Be thankful. "It is your attitude, not your aptitude, that determines your altitude" is a quote attributed to Zig Ziglar, a well-known motivational speaker and author. Ziglar was famous for his teachings on personal development, success, and positive thinking.

    Have an attitude of gratitude and a positive outlook on life will create opportunities beyond your imagination.

△

Prayer Partnerships

Prayer Partnerships - cultivate relationships with trusted prayer partners who can journey with you in silence, interceding together and bearing each other's burdens. (Galatians 6:2 *Carry one another's burdens; in this way you will fulfill the law of Christ.*)

Being involved in corporate worship settings, Sunday services, weekday services, small Bible study groups, prayer groups, to name a few, allows you to meet men and women who are also seeking the Lordship of Jesus Christ in their lives. Developing trust in these settings as well as finding kindred spirits allow the doors to open to your hearts to share prayer requests and pray for each other. It also allows you to SEE what God is doing in each other's lives as you see answers to your prayers. You can rejoice with these believers as they rejoice with you.

Recognize that people are sometimes in your life for a "season." This season may be days, weeks, months or years. This season may be continually or spread out over time. Knowing that sharing your requests now doesn't mean you will always share with these people whenever you have a request. God brings people into your life for a reason, His reasons. You may not ever know this side of heaven why they were in your life— for you or for them—just know that God placed them there.

Cherish each prayer relationship in which you find yourself. Honor God in every way as you pray intentionally and sincerely for this person or these persons.

△

Unplanned Moments

Unplanned Moments — embrace moments of unexpected silence throughout your day, whether waiting in line, sitting in traffic, or pausing between tasks.

Example: Heading to meet some youth girls at church for a trip to a conference, I wanted a few minutes to be early to the church before we left to stop and relax in His Presence. Traffic stopped on the interstate bridge. I had no where to go. I had to just sit and wait for the traffic issue to be solved. God gave me 45 minutes to laugh with Him, in His Presence, in my car, waiting as I was trying to get to the church!

God was so good that day! He was talking to me in an unplanned moment. It was an unexpected time of silence in my day and it proved to be the best use of my time as I was waiting in my car.

What is happening in your day? Become aware of moments that God can use for you to listen to His still, small voice. In the past I've used a traffic light picture to remind me to "Stop, Drop, Pray" - Red, Yellow (Kneel), Green! Carry this image in your mind so you can develop this tool to enjoy each moment of every day.

Bertha Smith was a missionary in China at the turn of the century, 1900's (that century). She told me when I was a teenager to focus on "praying without ceasing!" She said that if I would always be ready to pray, always be looking for God to speak to me, then I would be more likely to hear Him when was speaking and be ready to pray for those He brought to my mind. These unplanned moments are ones that God can use to develop our character in Christ—*Make your own attitude that of Christ Jesus.* CSB. Or *Let this mind be in you which was also in Christ Jesus.* NKJV

    Let these moments which can come at anytime day or night bring light for the darkness that surrounds us every day. Be ready to be different from the world around us during this moments so we can experience God's full Presence in

His glory and grace. He has so much He wants to share with us each day and sometimes we are just too busy to stop and see it. Be more mindful of the moments He offers you today.

△

Holy Listening

Holy Listening: Practice the art of listening prayer, quieting your own thoughts, and attentively listening for God's voice speaking to you in the depths of your heart.

What was the last thing you heard God telling you in His still, small voice? Focus in on that thought, those words. Ask Him to speak to you in the depths of your heart.   Listen quietly to His voice. What do you hear?   What phrases or songs or psalms or verses does He bring to mind?   What have you been studying recently in His Word? Is there a theme in what you've been hearing from Him?

Actively listen for God to speak. He is holy. We are made holy through the gift of God through Christ Jesus. *Bless the Lord, O my soul; and all that is within me, bless His holy name."* Psalm 103:1 CSB

You have made known to me the ways of life; You will make me full of joy in Your Presence. Acts 2:28. CSB

1 Peter 1:13-16. *Therefore, with your minds ready for action, be serious and set your hope completely on the grace to be brought to you at the revelation of Jesus Christ. As obedient children, do not be conformed to the desires of your former ignorance. But as the One who called you is holy, you also are to be holy in all your*

conduct; for it is written, Be holy, because I am holy. 1 Peter 1:13-16 CSB

△

Reflect on Your Day

Reflect on your day: Evening time brings opportunities for gratitude and honesty, inviting God to reveal His Presence and guidance in the midst of your joys and strengths for the day.

- What did God do in your life today?

- What were your victories?

- Did you share the victories with a prayer partner to encourage them?

- Where did He show up unexpectedly? Are you doing this: *Being silent before the Lord and waiting expectantly for Him?* [OOOO! That is what this is all about!]

▸ Where was He waiting for you as you went about your day?

▸ Are you ready to tell Him how grateful you are?

▸ Be honest with God about how are you are at this moment, at the end of your day.

▸ Be sensitive to the whisper from your heavenly Father who wants to fill you with His joy as you close out today knowing tomorrow is in His control already.

△

Digital Sunset Ritual

Digital Sunset Ritual: Establish a daily ritual of turning off screens and electronic devices at sunset, symbolizing a transition into rest and a space for evening prayer and reflections.

Go outside and watch the physical sunset. Notice the colors. Observe the cloud formations around the sun. Listen for the quietness that nature offers at this transition from day to night.

Take a moment when you are in a new place for the evening to find the sunset at the end of the day and enjoy the beauty that is set before you. Be aware again of the colors, the clouds, the quietness around you.

    Pausing from our digital world in which we find ourselves daily, can allow you to dwell in His Presence even more.

    Pause for God to speak.

    Pause for God to hear your gratitude.

    Pause to know Him better.

    Pause to sit in silence in His Presence....

△

What do I do next?

Try the tools that work best of you!

One of my favorite remembrances of God meeting me in the stillness of the day came years ago. I was kneeling at my open window on a summer evening. I told God I did not "feel" Him.

He reminded me that His Word doesn't say I will "feel" Him. It says in He promises that He will always be with me. I can trust He will be there for me. I told Him I was going to sit

there until I felt His Presence. Immediately I was startled by a lightning bug. God whispered "I am the Light of the world." When I accepted Jesus into my life, He came to stay with me from that day forward.
Because He lives in me, I am to be His light to the world around me. I am like the lightning bug. I am to shine His light to the world.

    I looked out into the backyard and there were lots of lightning bugs filling the yard. I was so grateful that God had chosen me and provided for me the presence of lightning bugs to remind me that He will always be with me.

Look forward to being silent in His Presence as you begin to include more of these moments of silence in your daily walk with the Father.

May God bless you in every area of your life as you seek His face first! Matthew 6:33, *"Seek first the kingdom of God and His righteousness, and all these things will be provided for you."* CSB

Psalm 37:7
Be silent before the Lord
and wait expectantly for Him.

△

Join us for more conversations...

www.InHisFaithfulness.com

www.InHisRest.com

△

Your thoughts...

Your thoughts...

Your thoughts...